Paul Poiret at age 30,
in 1909.

Poiret's travel outfit for a fashion tour to
Denmark, 1926.

Plate 1

Union suit, so called because it unified the top garment with the bottom, 1909.

Girdle of mercerized brocade with front lacing and lace trim, worn with white batiste camisole top, 1918.

Plate 2

An early creation for
Jacques Doucet, 1896.

Costume for Sarah Bernhardt in
Queen Elizabeth, 1912.

Plate 3

Evening gown, 1908.

"Carotte" (carrot), summer dress, 1909.

Plate 4

Coat, from a film of Poiret's collection
used to illustrate his lectures on fashion
design, 1910.

Pantaloon gown, 1911.

Plate 5

Fur-trimmed gown, 1911.

"Sorbet," Poiret's famous lampshade tunic (influenced by Léon Bakst's costumes for Diaghilev's Ballets Russes) of satin with pearl embroidery, 1912.

Plate 6

Costume inspired by the gardens
of Versailles, 1913.

Costume for Mata Hari in
Le Minaret, 1913.

Plate 7

"Tuileries," duvetyn suit, 1913.

Evening gown with embroidered skirt, 1914.

Plate 8

"Bénévole," duvetyn dress and cape, with the velvet lining of the cape forming a muffler, 1917.

"Faune" (faun), evening gown with backless bodice, gold lamé turban, and skirt of monkey fur intermingled with gold fringe, 1919.

Plate 9

September 24, 2019

To whom it may concern,

Please be advised that Clarita Crisostoma, mother of For-mari, was a patient at Nathan Adelson Hospice, located at 4141 Swenson Street, Las Vegas, Nevada, 89119. Nathan Adelson Hospice is an organization dedicated to the care of patients who are terminally ill. She was admitted to our inpatient unit on September 19, 2019 and expired on September 24, 2019. We encourage quality of life and opportunities to spend time with family and friends, which is so beneficial to anticipatory grief and bereavement needs. We believe their presence at this time is of great value to the patient, and for emotional support to the rest of the family. Ms. Crisostoma is requesting assistance in adjustment of her travel arrangements so she may be with her family during this difficult time.

Please contact Nathan Adelson Hospice (702) 733.0320 if further information is required.

Sincerely,

Warren Wheeler, MD

Senior Medical Director

Nathan Adelson Hospice

4141 SWENSON STREET
LAS VEGAS, NEVADA 89119
702.733.0320
FAX 702.938.3900

3150 N. TENAYA WAY, SUITE 350
LAS VEGAS, NEVADA 89128
702.733.0320
FAX 702.724.9323

2270 E. COMMERCIAL ROAD, SUITE A/B
PAHRUMP, NEVADA 89048
775.751.6700
FAX 775.751.5651

Coat of wool and silk blend trimmed with
pierced white leather (not lace), with
ermine collar, 1918.

Bare-midriff evening gown designed for
the actress Spinelly, with fabric designed
by Raoul Dufy and inspired by the
bandana, 1919.

Plate 10

Traveling costume designed for Spinelly
for a trip to the United States, 1920.

Tulle and taffeta dress, 1921.

Plate 11

Crêpe dress with embroidery, 1922.

Evening ensemble in velvet trimmed
with fur and embroidery, 1922.

Plate 12

"Colibri" (hummingbird), tunic of embroidered crêpe du Maroc with crêpe
skirt, 1923.

Evening dress veiled with patterned
lace, 1923.

Plate 13

"Soldat" (soldier), wool tailor-made, 1924.

"Le Rhin" (the Rhine), velvet evening dress embroidered with silver and veiled with lace, 1924.

Plate 14

Day dress, 1925.

Evening dress of the fabric "Coquillages"
(seashells) designed by Raoul Dufy, 1925.

Plate 15

Crêpe de Chine day dress with hand-
painted designs, 1926.

"Beau Masque," tulle evening gown
embroidered in chenille, 1929.

Plate 16